Please Ignore
SERVICE DOGS

Please Ignore
SERVICE DOGS

CATHERINE PFEIFER, PH.D.
ILLUSTRATIONS BY KARLA NEMITZ

Please Ignore Service Dogs

Catherine Pfeifer, PhD

FIRST EDITION

ISBN: 979-8-9857858-0-7
eBook ISBN: 979-8-9857858-1-4

Library of Congress Control Number: 2022933090

© 2022 Catherine Pfeifer

MP
Merganser Press

Acknowledgments

Thank you to the following:
Jerry Payne
Can Do Canines
Alan Peters
Jane Thompson
Robert Vaughn
Terri Krake and Brody
Jane Berliss-Vincent
Red Bird/Red Oak Writing
Sarah Whitney
Dave Neumann
Sarah Shiff
Amy (Zing) Gray
Antonia Levi
Waldo Sheboygan
(Yes, that really is the cat's name. It's funnier if you are
from Wisconsin and have driven north on Highway 43.)
And, of course, Paul and Nina.

Contents

Welcome to the World of the Service Dog   **1**

Guide Dogs   5

Hearing Assist Dogs   7

Diabetic Alert Dogs   17

Seizure Response Dogs   19

Autism Assist Dogs   23

Mobility Assist Dogs   25

Psychiatric Disabilities Assist Dogs   27

Special Skills Service Dogs   31

Dogs that aren't Service Dogs   32

Training   **40**

**More about Nina: Service Dog,
but Dog Nonetheless**   **42**

A Typical Day in the Life of Nina the Service Dog   46

Some Other Things about Nina
(or Any Service Dog, for that Matter)   50

**Some Interesting ADA Stuff If You Happen
to Own a Business**   **53**

Please Ignore Service Dogs   **56**

Types of Distractors   **60**

Frequently Asked Questions   71

A Transition in Three Conversations   85

Bibliography and Recommended Books   89

Welcome to the World of the Service Dog

Okay, so what *is* a service dog, anyway? Service dogs are specifically trained to perform necessary services that allow their human partners to live in a safer manner. They're a necessary factor in allowing their partners to live independently, and even though a service dog might be the same species as your companion animal, he's also very different. Your pet might be a great comfort to you, and you might love your pet very much (and no doubt your pet loves you right back), but your pet isn't providing services that are indispensable. Sure, maybe in the grander scheme of things love is indispensable, but let's take, for instance, a diabetic alert dog. This is a dog that will detect a drop in his partner's blood sugar and warn them of the impending issue, which will allow the partner to take action before there's a medical emergency. We're talking potential life-saving activity here. *That's* a service dog. There is one way you can help a service dog do their job: ignore them!

"Service dog" is a title. A job description. Not just any good boy or girl qualifies. A service dog is actually a very specific term, as defined by the Americans with Disabilities Act (ADA) 2010 Revised Requirements:

"Service animals are defined as dogs which are individually trained to do work or perform tasks for people with disabilities. Examples of such work or tasks include: guiding people who are blind; alerting people who are deaf; pulling a wheelchair; alerting and protecting a person who is having a seizure; reminding a person with mental illness to take prescribed medications; calming a person with Post Traumatic Stress Disorder (PTSD) during an anxiety attack, or performing other duties…Service animals are working animals, not pets. The work or task a dog has been trained to provide must be directly related to the person's disability. Dogs whose sole function is to provide comfort or emotional support do not qualify as service animals under the ADA."[1]

There are other types of helpful dogs, of course, dogs not necessarily trained and working in accordance with the above definition, but that provide a relevant service nonetheless. A therapy dog, for instance, is a dog trained to be affectionate and comforting to people in institutional settings, like hospitals, retirement communities, nursing facilities, hospices, universities, and disaster-response scenes. You may have heard the term "facility dog" or "companion dog," which you'll also find in such settings. "Working dog" is an informal term you might have heard for dogs trained to perform specific tasks to aid or even to entertain. Watching a poodle play piano in Paris? Then you're enjoying the music of a working dog (though his father would have probably wished he'd have gone into doggie medicine or doggie law).

In some countries, the term "working dog" refers to dogs who manage livestock. The American Kennel Club defines working dogs as dogs who perform tasks other than hunting or herding. Working dogs can be sled dogs, guard dogs, sports dogs, police dogs, and detection dogs, which look for things like illegal drugs, explosives, or even bedbugs.

---

[1] Americans with Disabilities Act (ADA) 2010 Revised Requirements, U.S. Department of Justice, Civil Rights Division, Disability Rights Section, July 2011.

"Service dog" is more commonly used in the U.S. to refer to any type of dog that provides assistance with mobility, hearing alert, type 1 diabetes alert, psychiatric, navigation, and other needs. Historically, the term most commonly refers to guide dogs and mobility assistance dogs. Outside the U.S., the term "service dog" means a dog who works for police, military, or search and rescue services. In this book, we'll use service dog and assistance dog interchangeably, but the larger meaning is the same: a dog that is individually trained to do work or perform tasks for someone with a disability. Service (or assistance) dogs are certainly working dogs, but working dogs are not necessarily service dogs.

As it happens, there are many different types of service dogs. For example, there are guide dogs (or seeing-assist dogs), hearing assist dogs, the aforementioned diabetes dogs, seizure response dogs, autism assist dogs, mobility assist dogs, psychiatric disabilities dogs, and others. Let's consider some of these in a little more depth in the following sections.

Guide Dogs

These are the service dogs most people are familiar with. Guide dogs are trained to lead blind and visually impaired people around obstacles. They're directed by their human partner after the pair has gone through extensive training.

Guide Dog Story

Teresa, who is blind, was out taking a morning walk after an especially severe storm the night before. Her guide dog Gatsby, a golden retriever, was faithfully by her side as they traversed their usual route around the neighborhood. Suddenly, Gatsby stopped and pulled hard on his leash, ultimately walking Teresa twenty feet out of her way. Teresa had no idea why. She hadn't heard any cars or footsteps or anything that might indicate an obstruction in the road. Later, talking to a neighbor, she learned that the night before, the road had been flooded by the storm and a big chunk had been washed out. The road circled around a steep hill and had Teresa stepped into the hole that the storm had left behind, she would have slipped several hundred yards down a slope of mud and rock. Gatsby had seen the danger and walked Teresa safely around it. Now *that's* a guide dog!

And here's the thing about Gatsby. Like any good guide dog, he was trained in something called "intelligent disobedience." This means that Teresa could have pulled on his leash all she wanted and insisted—even commanded—Gatsby to continue through their usual route. But Gatsby would have intentionally held his ground, keeping Teresa safe no matter what commands she would have given him. This type of "disobedience" was taught during his training to reinforce safety over the cues of his handler.

Hearing Assist Dogs

Hearing assist dogs alert a deaf or hard-of-hearing person to sounds by making physical contact with her, then leading her to the source of the sound. Sounds the dog may be trained for include doorbells, clock alarms, smoke detector alarms, telephone rings, a baby's cry, a door knock, a voice calling the partner's name, or the sound of an intruder.

Learning about Hearing Assist Dogs

One day I was in the grocery store with my mother. While I was picking up some items, Mom made her way over to the meat counter, where I soon spotted her talking to a tall, beautifully dressed woman holding a leash attached to a corgi. The dog wore the typically exuberant corgi expression and a bright red vest. Mom collected her package of meat from the butcher and came over to me.

"Did you talk to that lady?" I asked. "What did she say?"

"I talked to her but she didn't answer," Mom said.

"I'm going to go over and ask her about her dog. I think it's a service dog."

"Don't you dare ask to pet her dog," Mom pre-scolded. "It's obviously working."

"Please give me a little credit, Mom," I replied, post-mortified. "I *am* over fifty."

I walked over to the woman's side and said hello but the woman didn't reply. She completely ignored me, in fact. I stood there awkwardly trying to decide whether or not to tap her shoulder when I saw the dog nudge her leg. At that, the woman turned around.

"'Lo," she said. Then she reached into her pocket and gave the dog a treat. The corgi stared blissfully at her.

"I am sorry to interrupt you," I said, pointing at her dog, "but what type of service does your dog provide?"

"I am deaf, and he is my service dog," she said.

"What exactly does he do?" I asked.

"He alerts me when there are important sounds, like the smoke detector," she replied.

"Where did you get him?" I asked.

"I'm from Alaska and got him there. I just moved to Milwaukee. I don't know any service dog trainers in this area."

I looked down at the dog. He had a patch on his vest that announced, "Hearing Assist Dog" and another that requested, "Do not pet me, I am working."

I thanked the woman, and returned to my mom. "Please remember the words 'Hearing Assist Dog'," I said. "I need to look those up when we get home." We finished the rest of the grocery shopping while I chanted *hearing assist dog, hearing assist dog, hearing assist dog,* so I wouldn't forget.

I didn't forget.

Once home, I launched a week-long research project, investigating service dogs, hearing assist dogs, and everything else about the topic I could uncover.

When I tell people this story, they often ask how this woman knew what I was saying. "You told me that she was deaf," they say. After going out in public with my husband Paul and his hearing assist dog, I can predict what people are going to say or ask us about Paul's service dog with amazing accuracy. In fact, it's because of Paul's hearing loss that I became so interested in service dogs in the first place. You'll learn more about Paul and his dog as the book continues. The point is, just like the deaf woman in the store, I know very well what people are going to ask us. Our answers have almost turned into a patter song—basically the contents of this book—that we repeat over and over.

Here's an actual patter song that we might consider using:

This is the very model of a modern service animal.
She helps me navigate my day with expertise methodical.
She knows her job and concentrates with application dutiful.
So please do not distract her, even though you think she's beautiful.

Hearing Assist Dog Story

Mario lives alone in his two-story house and is deaf. He relies on his dog Nicky to alert him to important sounds he cannot hear. She tells him when the doorbell rings, when the phone rings, and when someone pulls up in his driveway. One night, she woke Mario from a deep sleep. He looked over at the clock: 3:13 a.m. The phone hadn't rung, and it was a strange time for anybody to be ringing the bell or pulling up to the house. Mario rose and began walking downstairs to the front door, but Nicky pawed his leg and ran the other way toward the living room window that looked out on the backyard. Mario followed and peered through the window blinds to see someone walking around. A prowler was on the property. Mario called 9-1-1 and within a few minutes, the police showed up. The prowler took off into the woods behind the property, and Mario hasn't seen him since. He'll never know the prowler's intentions, but he sleeps better knowing that any unusual sound around the house, not just doorbells, phones, or approaching cars, will be heard by Nicky and Nicky will let Mario know about it.

Paul's Story

Who's Paul? He's my husband, and he's deaf. We met in 2009 and on our first date, while playing Dating Chicken, I learned that he developed some hearing loss in 2002 after flying home from a European vacation with a sinus infection. His ears popped, which is common during flights, but it damaged the cilia in Paul's ears, which is definitely not common. Paul went to a hearing specialist, who confirmed his hearing loss. His hearing has been declining since then.

What is Dating Chicken? It's a technique I developed in my thirties to determine whether it's worthwhile for a couple to go on a second date. The rules are simple: tell the truth about yourself and let the other party decide if it's a deal-breaker. We had a Dating Chicken conversation about animals, and it went something like this:

Cate: I have a rescue cat named Ginger. She was severely traumatized before I got her. If you pick her up, she will piss on you. I'm not talking a tiny trickling stream. I'm talking torrential downpour. I'm talking piss-ageddon. A piss-acolypse. A category five tropical piss-storm. If you want to hold her, bring a change of clothes.

Paul: Holy cow! Is she okay? What happened to her?

Cate: I don't know. When I went to the shelter to find a cat, I asked to use the toilet. The attendant at the shelter warned me the cat that guarded the commode was irritated by the entire world. When I walked into the bathroom, I found an angry cat dominating two timid cats who had dared invade her tiled turf. I sat and listened as the angry cat tried to calm herself with purring in between growling, spitting, and hissing. She sounded like an old car trying to start on a sub-zero morning. There were lots of spurts and sputters between the grinding sounds. I knew she was trying so hard to calm herself but she couldn't do it in the shelter. So I took her home.

Paul: You adopted the angriest cat in the world?

Cate: Let's just say she's the most traumatized cat in a three-state area.

Paul: Why would you adopt a cat like that?

Cate: She needed a friend. She needed to be rescued from the shelter. Anyway, I took Ginger home, then didn't see her for six months. I knew she was there because while I slept, the food disappeared and the litter box filled. But one day I awoke to find her sleeping on the very edge of the bed. After another half-year she let me pet her. A half-year later, she started to purr when I petted her. Now she sleeps on the bed every night. Is my pissy cat a deal breaker?

Paul: Not at all. I love animals. I have a dog named Chief. A black lab. He sleeps with me every night.

Cate: Cool. Does your dog hunt?

Paul: No. His only job is to be my best friend. I hope you like dogs.

Cate: Very much.

Paul: Good, because that would be a deal-breaker if you didn't. Just to be clear, if you stay over, he will sleep in the middle of the bed. I hope Chief likes you.

Cate: Another deal breaker?

Paul: Absolutely. Big time.

About a year after this conversation Chief died from cancer. Shortly thereafter Ginger died from sudden onset feline diabetes. I adopted a mated pair of cats, and Paul moved in with me. Any talk of getting a new dog resulted in the same three-point discussion.

First, Paul always claimed it was too soon to get another dog after Chief.

Second, Chief was Paul's best friend ever. All other dogs would pale in comparison to this epic bromance. Paul and Chief had the greatest friendship since Robin Hood and Little John. Abbott and Costello? Or was it Bonnie and Clyde? I forget which comparison was used.

The third was that the condo board did not allow dogs. In fact, the rules allowed only one cat per unit, but my neighbors had graciously forgotten to tattle on me. My new cats were adorable, social, playful, and did not have a "Burn in hell, biped," expression stuck on their faces.

One day I got a call from my mother, who asked me to come over to fix her iPad. Paul and I had just ordered a pizza to have for our dinner and so I asked Paul to wait for the pizza while I went to help Mom. I quickly walked the three blocks to her place, reset her iPad, and went home. On my return I noticed Paul had turned a chair to look out the window at the front steps. I asked him why. He confessed it was the only way he could tell if the pizza had arrived.

Paul has never heard my doorbell. The tone is too high for him to hear. Like so many hard-of-hearing people, Paul has been faking it beautifully for years. He's learned to read lips, use interpolation, apply guesswork, nod even if he can't hear what's being said, and read rooms for the reactions of others.

The truth is that no one can really read lips. Studies indicate that "Only about 30% to 45% of the English language is discernible through lip reading, while contextualization and guessing determine the remainder." (This is from a great article by C. Lieu and colleagues. Check out the citation in the bibliography.) Lip movement can be used as a cue to help a deaf or hard-of-hearing person guess what's being said, but there are a limited number of mouth shapes for a countless number of sounds. Reading lips does not help with the sounds made in our throat or inside the mouth. Some sounds made primarily using the teeth, tongue, and larynx cannot be seen. Plus, there can be other complicating factors in trying to read lips, like trying to decipher a mumbler or someone with a bushy mustache.

I approached the woman in the grocery store because I was especially interested in hearing assist dogs, realizing this could give Paul another way to navigate the world with his diminishing hearing. I knew Paul would be delighted if a four-legged best friend could go everywhere with him for the rest of his life. Paul would never forget Chief, of course, but he was ready to entertain the thought of another dog, especially one who could provide so much help. And so, we acquired Nina, a Labrador retriever trained to be a hearing assist dog. We also moved out of the condo so that Nina would have a yard to play in. Stay tuned. You'll learn more about Nina later.

Diabetic Alert Dogs

Diabetic alert dogs work with people who have type 1 diabetes with hypoglycemia unawareness, which is a complication of diabetes where the person doesn't feel the typical symptoms of a steep drop in blood sugar (hypoglycemia). Most people feel shakiness or dizziness, or perhaps anxiety. They may feel sweaty or get a sudden headache. If these symptoms aren't present, the person may have no idea that his or her blood sugar had fallen to a dangerous level.

The diabetic alert dog can detect a drop in blood sugar, alert the partner to their physiological change, bring the partner juice or some other sugar source, and get help or retrieve an emergency phone. Consequently, the situation can be addressed before it becomes dangerous.

Rest assured, diabetic alert dog training doesn't involve allowing a diabetic to get to dangerous levels with their blood glucose. Instead, while a client waits to be partnered with her assistance dog, she's given instructions on how to safely collect a scent sample for training purposes. The scent sample is used to teach the diabetic alert dog-in-training to use a behavior like a nose nudge to alert their handler when they smell that signal.

Diabetic Alert Dog Story

Gina has diabetes with hypoglycemia unawareness. Her service dog Harley was trained to discern Gina's hypoglycemia by noticing a change in Gina's breath that would indicate low blood sugar. When Harley picks up this particular scent, he nudges Gina's leg. One day, Gina fell asleep on her sofa watching television, only to have Harley wake her up by repeatedly nudging her leg. Gina felt fine and assumed Harley needed to go out. She moved towards the door, but Harley stayed in place. Gina shrugged and began walking towards the kitchen, but Harley followed her, nudging her leg several more times. Finally, Gina checked her blood sugar reading only to discover that it was at 58. Anything lower than 70 is cause for concern. Lower than 54 is critical. Gina drank a glass of juice, and in a few minutes her blood sugar stabilized. What could have been a dangerous situation turned out okay thanks to Harley, who was rewarded with a well-earned treat and a pat on the head.

Seizure Response Dogs

Seizure response dogs protect their partners during seizures and help them recover. These service dogs work with people who live with seizure disorders such as epilepsy. Besides finding help for someone experiencing a seizure, the dog can nudge or lick a person to help stimulate them and bring them back to consciousness after a seizure, rest against the person with their weight to keep the person still, or retrieve a phone or medication. Seizure response dogs might carry medicines with them or have patches that announce that information about the human is available in the service dog's pocket. They often know how to brace so that their human can use them if they feel unbalanced. They can also be trained to engage a nerve stimulator (as the following story illustrates), or run for help.

Some dogs are natural seizure *alert* dogs. They naturally alert to a seizure, although nobody really knows why. No one knows what cues they pick up on. You can't train a dog to alert to a seizure, but you can train a dog to *respond* to one.

Seizure Response Dog Story

Terri, who has lived with epilepsy, had grand mal epileptic seizures so intense they would cause her to be immobilized on the floor except for involuntary spasms. These seizures would typically go on for about forty minutes. She eventually got a Vagus Nerve Stimulator (VNS), which can be thought of as a pacemaker for the brain. This device sends an electrical impulse to the brain, which stops the seizures. Terri's VNS is programmed to fire automatically every five minutes so her seizures never last longer than that amount of time.

Brody is Terri's seizure assist dog, and he's able to alert to chemical changes in Terri that indicate a seizure is coming on. Once alerted by Brody, Terri will lie down, and Brody will climb on top of her and start to snuggle her. This is helpful in several ways. First, as Brody puts his nose against Terri's neck, a magnet in his collar ends up in the perfect position to trigger the VNS and stop the seizure within seconds. In fact, Brody can stop most seizures before they even begin. Second, by lying on top of Terri, Brody limits the involuntary seizure movements that might harm her. Finally, Brody provides a comforting focus to help Terri become aware of her surroundings as she regains consciousness.

Terri estimates that in one single year, Brody triggered her VNS fifty-five times. The year after that, one hundred. How amazing is that? Before Brody, Terri used to have anywhere from five to ten seizures a week. With Brody's help, that number is down to two or three a month. You can learn more about Terri and Brody in Maria Goodavage's book, *Doctor Dogs: How our Best Friends Are Becoming Our Best Medicine.*

Autism Assist Dogs

Autism assist dogs help families with autistic children. (They can assist with autistic adults, as well.) An autism assist dog can help an autistic child feel safe and secure. These dogs help their partners learn how to socialize, too. Other kids are naturally drawn to an autism assist dog, and they end up talking to the dog's partner—the autistic child. The presence of the dog also gives the human partner a popular topic to discuss (dogs!). Since people will often ask the same questions about the service dog, the autistic child gets a lot of practice answering them, thus giving him more confidence with his social interaction skills.

Some dogs are tethered to their autistic child partner. If the child tends to wander, the dog can reduce the chance of the child wandering off. The dog can lie down and become something of an anchor, allowing the child to roam no farther than the length of the leash. Or, if the child becomes agitated, the dog can lead the child to a quieter place where, by providing pressure therapy, she can help the child to re-engage with her surroundings. Also, simply by the dog's presence, the child is provided comfort in times of frustration.

Autism Assist Dog Story

Candice has a thirteen-year-old autistic son named Billy who has a tendency to take off in random directions when they're out in public. This is especially true at the grocery store, where he's been known to get out of the car and run across the parking lot, causing Candice no end of worry. Well, at least that's the way things *used* to be. Candice eventually acquired Tango, an autism assist dog that stays by Billy's side and keeps him calm and under control. Now, wherever they are, Billy walks calmly beside Tango, who leads him along, always making sure he doesn't run off by himself. Not only has Tango made things safer for Billy, but Billy loves his new friend and feels much more confident in his presence. Needless to say, Candice feels the same way!

Mobility Assist Dogs

Mobility assist dogs work with people who use wheel-chairs, walkers, or crutches and can be trained to help people with their needs. These dogs can open and close doors, pull wheelchairs or steady someone as they walk, turn lights on and off, help their partners pick up and carry objects, get help or retrieve an emergency phone, and perform more routine tasks.

The best thing a mobility assist dog might provide is peace of mind. If a person is unable to perform simple tasks for him or herself, such as standing up without help or picking something up off the floor (such as a pencil or even a credit card!), it's reassuring to know a service dog is there to help.

Mobility Assist Dog Story

Julio is paralyzed from the waist down and uses a wheel-chair. He relies on his service dog Ripley to accompany him when he's out and about, or to help with simple tasks around the house, like retrieving items—the TV remote, for example, or maybe the phone, or even a beer from the fridge (good Ripley!).

Julio has not one, but two amazing stories of when Ripley came to his rescue, possibly saving his life. The first was when Julio and Ripley were out for a walk one night. Julio's wheelchair tipped over when he was turning a corner. With his hands, he managed to right the chair, but he couldn't pull himself up onto it. Not to worry. Ripley was there to help brace Julio, giving Julio a rising surface to press against as Ripley essentially raised Julio up to where he could swing himself into the wheelchair. "It was late at night on a quiet street," says Julio. "I have no idea how long I would have been lying there. And it was getting colder, too."

The second instance was in the house. Julio's chair fell over, but this time he was awkwardly pinned against the wall with the wheelchair between him and Ripley. Ripley couldn't help Julio up, but he knew what to do just the same. He left the room and came back moments later with Julio's phone, which he was able to drop within arm's length. Julio dialed his neighbor for help, and all was right with the world. "He's my hero," Julio says of Ripley.

Psychiatric Disabilities
Assist Dogs

Psychiatric disabilities assist dogs work with people who have panic disorders, post-traumatic stress disorder (PTSD), depression, or other mental health issues. Now, any dog might offer comfort or a sense of security to a partner, but emotional support does not qualify as a "trained task" under the Americans with Disabilities Act. To be qualified to be a legal service dog, a psychiatric disabilities assist dog is trained to perform a medically-necessary task. These tasks might include reminding their partner to take medication, fetching the medication, fetching water, scouting a room for safety, retrieving an emergency phone, or using a pre-programmed dog-operated phone to deliver messages asking for help. That's right. I said dog-operated phone.

Psychiatric Disabilities Assist Dog Story

Sheri has spent most of her adult life dealing with panic attacks, the result of certain traumatic childhood incidents. The panic attacks are characterized by acute anxiety, sometimes leading to hyperventilation, and had reached a point where Sheri had become afraid of leaving her home. Then into the picture came Sasha, a trained psychiatric assist service dog. At first, Sasha helped Sheri tremendously with her panic attacks, sensing when one might be coming on. She knew the tell-tale signs—the rapid breathing and the increased heart rate. But somehow she knew even before these signs would manifest themselves. When she detected an oncoming attack, Sasha would bring Sheri medications and water. Sasha would then cuddle with Sheri until the medications took effect.

In time, however, Sasha came to mean even more freedom to Sheri. Accompanied by Sasha, who carried her medications and water, Sheri was able to leave her home for longer and longer periods of time. When Sheri was hesitant to enter a new environment, Sasha was there to scout ahead and reassure her. With Sasha by her side, Sheri felt safe and secure. Today, Sheri feels like she can function out in public, as long as she has Sasha by her side.

Special Skills Service Dogs

Special skills dogs provide assistance to people who have very specific needs. For example, the dog might be trained to identify by smell if a food item has an ingredient to which their partner has a deadly allergy. It might be that someone needs a special skills service dog if they're living with more than one disability.

Special Skills Service Dog Story

Desmond has chronic hypertension. Among other risk factors, his condition sometimes leads to sudden drops in blood pressure. These can result in fainting. That's where Brewster comes in. Brewster is a cardiac alert dog, trained to sense a sudden drop in Desmond's blood pressure long before Desmond can. Alerted to the impending drop, Desmond can take his prescribed medication and lie down and rest until the situation stabilizes, no fainting involved. You might say Desmond has a special place in his heart for Brewster.

Dogs that aren't Service Dogs

Earlier, we talked about the Americans with Disabilities Act (ADA) and the legal definition of "service dog." But from a practical standpoint, how does an otherwise normal dog become a service dog? The short answer is through consistent and constant training. An excellent way to get service dog training is through an *accredited training facility*. The major accreditation organization is Assistance Dogs International. ADI is a nonprofit organization whose purpose is to improve the areas of training, placement, and utilization of service dogs. Nina, Paul's service dog, for example, was trained at Can Do Canines, an ADI-accredited training organization. ADI has a comprehensive accreditation system, and becoming a chapter member is not an easy task. Once acquired, membership needs to be maintained by staying current with every new requirement. Accredited organizations are regularly assessed to ensure they meet the high standards expected of service dog programs.

Some people chose to obtain their service dog

through an independent service dog trainer, or train their dog themselves. No matter where it was trained, if the dog is obedient and controlled in public while performing trained tasks that mitigate his handler's disability, then it is a service dog.

Keep in mind, however, that even an expertly trained service dog can have a bad day. The dog might be sick and relieve itself in a building. Maybe it's distracted and misses a cue. If a dog is unruly, service dog or not, a business owner or other authority figure can ask the handler to remove the dog from the premises. Under the ADA, the handler is entitled to return, but without the dog.

Fortunately, bad days are rare for well-trained service dogs, but there are many fraudulent owner/animal teams out there that make things difficult for real service animals. Some people have a tendency to want to bring their pets with them wherever they go, and one way to do so is to claim that the pet is a service dog. How can you tell a faker? That's the dog in the restaurant that's barking or relieving himself in the corner or eating off another patron's plate. The dog is *untrained*, in other words, and no more a service animal than, say, a pet duck.

Hey, this is no idle comparison. A passenger on an airplane flight once tried to bring her duck aboard the plane claiming it was an emotional support animal. This happens more than you think. There have been stories of peacocks, pigs, hamsters, goats, and even spiders showing up with their owners at airports and being claimed as necessary. Some may legitimately be claimed as emotional support animals. Most cannot. I suspect the owners of most of these animals were trying to game the airlines so they wouldn't have to pay expensive animal shipping rates. Maybe they felt the pet was safer in the cabin. Whatever the reason, it reflects poorly on people who rely on real service animals so that they can function day to day.

It should be noted that the Air Carrier Access Act, put in place to prohibit discrimination on the basis of disability in air travel, uses a different definitional standard for assistance dog than the Americans with Disabilities Act, but both laws protect all parties involved. The laws regarding animals on airplanes are changing faster than we can document here.

What to do about Service Animal Fakery

A friend of ours recently called a coffeehouse to ask if she could bring her pet dog inside. The barista told her the dog would indeed be welcome. She also matter-of-factly told my friend that if anyone challenged her about her dog's presence, she should just say it's a service dog. She said it like it was standard operational procedure at the coffeehouse. I mention this little story as proof that the fake service animal problem is more pervasive than you might believe. Now, finding a way to skirt the normal rules to bring your dog with you into a public place might not seem egregious. But it's no different, really, than any of the other ways that people fake disabilities for their own gain or convenience: fake disability parking tags, fake worker compensation claims, government disability fraud, even students faking a disability to get more time to take tests and finish homework. Not only do these deceptions rob resources from people who honestly need them, but it makes the public suspicious of those who need help.

So what to do? Well, it's tempting to seek ways to clearly identify a legal service animal so that even the untrained eye can spot a fake. How about a special vest? you ask. No doubt you've seen service dogs with special vests. The problem is, you can go on Amazon and for about twenty dollars, you can have your choice of bogus "Service Dog" vests. You can even get specific vests that say, "Therapy Service Dog" (Wait! That makes no sense.) or "PTSD." They come in all shapes and sizes to fit a Chihuahua to a Great Dane. All kinds of colors, too. So, basically, a vest means nothing.

How about if we registered service animals so that they came with papers that a person would be required to show if he or she was getting on an airplane or bringing an animal into a restaurant? Bad idea! People with service dogs don't want to go through Checkpoint Charlie at every door. It's akin to having to constantly prove that they have a disability. They don't want to be regarded as The Other any more than they already are. They just want to do ordinary things as simply as possible. Just like everyone else.

Think of it this way: Service dogs are legally designated as medical equipment. Do we want to start asking people in wheelchairs if they have the proper registration? Hey, blind person, do you have a license to carry around that white cane? Plus, it's just another burden, something else to have to remember. Take Paul, for example. He has cochlear implants, which help him perceive sound, and the batteries last anywhere between four to eight hours. Even though Paul has a great memory, he's been known to forget his batteries once in a while. Like any person leaving his house, he already has to remember his keys, wallet, glasses, and everything he needs for Nina including her doggy diaper bag, leash, and food. Do we really need to add something else? Requiring paperwork that someone has to bring along with their service dog just adds to a disabled person's already complicated life.

Believe it or not, we've even had ordinary people walk up to us demanding proof that Nina is a service dog. Not grocery store managers or employees, mind you. Just random strangers with apparent animal control issues.

The only real solution is *awareness*: making people aware that not all animals posing as service animals are service animals, and making people aware that posing one's pet as a service animal is not a victimless crime. It might make things more convenient, but it does so at the cost of credibility for people with real disabilities and real service animals. When someone pretends their pet is a service animal at the airport and the animal bites someone, the airlines are forced to add another level of paperwork for the protection of all passengers. Prices go up for all of us, and people with disabilities are forced to jump through another administrative hoop to get the services they need.

Do you know someone who has tried to pass off their dog as a service dog? Ask them not to do it. Ask them to please move out of the metaphorical disabled parking spot. Remember: every fake service animal is really a person faking a disability for personal convenience and using their animal for an inexcusable reason.

But back to the good guys...

Training

So what goes into the making of a service dog anyway? First of all, not every dog can be one. A good candidate possesses certain traits, such as intelligence, calmness, and a high work ethic. An assistance dog must be resilient, compliant, confident, and engaged before it can learn certain skills that would legally make it considered an assistance dog. At Can Do Canines in New Hope, Minnesota, the organization that trained Paul's service dog Nina, they breed some of their own dogs, usually black labs. They also acquire some of their dogs from breeders who donate them, and they get a few dogs from rescue shelters.

A service dog's training starts shortly after it is born. After the dog learns to walk, it will start wearing a tiny little vest to become comfortable with it. In the first year of a service dog's life there is an emphasis on socialization with humans and other dogs, name recognition, navigation of both unusual and common terrains (stairs and elevators, for example), exposure to new environments so that the dog can learn to stay calm with changes, basic commands such as sit, and leash obedience. In the second year, the dog focuses on advanced skills that would mitigate a future partner's disability.

Interestingly, the dog is not the only one in the partnership that's trained. The human partner is, too. Paul and I had to attend a week-long training course when we picked Nina up. They asked that the entire family become involved. Then we both worked with a local trainer until Paul and Nina were ready to graduate as a service *team*. (To this day, Nina remains much better trained than we are.)

More about Nina: Service Dog, but Dog Nonetheless

Paul's dog Nina presents us with a pretty decent case study of a real service dog. It's important to remember that Nina is an animal. Paul repeats this like a mantra: "Nina is a service dog, emphasis on *dog*." Nina is not a machine. She has the doggy equivalent of a PhD, but she is not a robot.

A few months after we got her, Paul's family and I went to the water park in the Wisconsin Dells. The park's staff knew about service dogs and were happy to accommodate Nina. In one of the restaurants, Nina walked into the room, shoved her nose deep into the carpet, and ecstatically started licking it. Paul tried everything to redirect her. Nothing worked. When he took her out of the room the behavior stopped. When they returned, she started again. Every time we walked past that restaurant,

Nina pulled on her leash to go in. Your guess is as good as ours as to why their rug was so damned delicious.

Nina doesn't like to get wet. If her tennis ball lands in water, she will stare at it until someone retrieves it for her. Oddly, she loves snow and will roll around in it all day. During sign-language classes, Nina falls asleep and makes little yipping noises with twitching running feet. She will fart or release a hilarious full-body sneeze during events when it is important for us to appear to be adults. She will occasionally try to befriend cats (even though she was trained to ignore them) and loves to steal their catnip toys. She does frenzied dances that rival Broadway musicals when feeding time approaches. She is, indeed, a dog.

Paul and I disagree whether Nina knows that Paul is deaf. Paul claims that Nina is more responsive when he is not wearing his cochlear implants. He believes that she knows when he can't hear. I believe that Nina has no idea Paul is deaf or, for that matter, that most people can hear. Dogs aren't capable of comprehending the lack of ability in a human. It takes a high level of intelligence and self-awareness to understand how another being experiences the world. There's no evidence that dogs can reflect on another's level of consciousness or perception, or, for that matter, on their own level of consciousness or perception. (Then again, we can always wax philosophical by asking, "Can anyone *really* know what a dog knows?")

Like all service dogs, Nina's service value is all in her training. Behavioral conditioning taught Nina that when she hears a particular sound (for example, a smoke detector), she needs to perform a certain action. In Nina's case, it's to give Paul a nudge with her nose. When Paul responds with a particular command—the palms up hand gesture and the verbal command "show me"—then, because of her training, Nina will lead him to the sound. Paul will reward her with a treat. It seems like a lot of work to do for irregularly timed snacks, but this cause-and-effect conditioning is all Nina knows about Paul's hearing loss.

As well-trained as she is, Nina also doesn't understand sign language, even though we're often asked if she does. Paul and I happen to be taking ASL (American Sign Language) classes so that we can keep every possible line of communication open. And even though Nina is attending these classes with us, she is showing a marked reluctance to do the homework, take exams, or even stay awake during class. She does have her own ASL name sign but she does not know what it means. She also doesn't know the custom-made ASL sign which signifies the mooing sounds she makes as she relaxes before drifting off to sleep. I created the latter sign in the class because the students always start laughing when Nina begins her mooing. By signing it in class, all the students clue our deaf ASL teacher in as to why they are giggling.

But even though dogs don't know ASL, animal trainers will pair certain hand gestures with the commands they teach their dogs. These are fairly consistent among dog trainers who train dogs for show, service, military, police, or agricultural purposes. Common dog commands with hand signals include sit, stay, down, and shake. Nina knows the hand signals for common dog commands, and she also knows a few designed just for hearing assist dogs. For example, she knows the palms-up "show me" gesture, and she also knows that tapping your leg means "nudge."

The service part of Nina's job helps Paul get through each day. She warns him of the sounds he needs to know about. She is also attentive to the people around them, making it unlikely for anyone to walk up behind Paul and startle him. But the dog part of her job is also important. Like everyone on this planet, Nina's not perfect. She makes us laugh every day, mostly with general dog goofiness and mooing sounds. Most importantly, she shows Paul that he doesn't have to face his silent world alone.

A Typical Day in the Life of Nina the Service Dog

So, what's a typical day like for Nina? It's a lot like this:

Morning

6:00 a.m.: Nina wakes up in our bed and starts to nudge Paul to give her breakfast.

6:15 a.m.: Nina has breakfast. Three-quarters of a cup of Kibble. Paul refreshes her water bowl.

6:25 a.m.: Nina goes out to our fenced-in backyard to sniff around and patrol. Paul cleans Nina's feet when she comes back in, the doggy equivalent of removing your shoes in the house.

6:35 a.m.: Nina returns to bed and waits for Paul to get ready for work.

7:30 a.m.: Nina follows Paul downstairs. He has breakfast. (It's not Kibble.)

8:00 a.m.: Paul puts Nina's collar, service-dog bandana, and tags on her. He makes sure her doggie bag has enough poop bags and dog reward treats.

8:10 a.m.: Paul buckles Nina into the back seat using her doggie seat belt. Nina wears a seat belt all the time she's in the car. She's never left alone in the car.

8:30 a.m.: Nina and Paul arrive at work.

9:00 a.m.: Nina follows Paul to meetings and around the office. When Paul is working, Nina rests on a dog mat next to his desk.

9:30 a.m.: Paul's phone rings. Nina alerts Paul by nudging him. After being nudged, Paul says, "Show me." Nina puts her paws on the desk and touches her nose to the phone. Paul rewards Nina. Nina then goes back to her mat.

10:15 a.m.: Paul gets an unexpected visitor. Nina hears the noise in the hall and alerts Paul by nudging him. After being nudged, Paul says, "Show me." Nina leads Paul to the hallway. Paul rewards Nina. Nina then goes back to her mat.

Afternoon

12:00 noon: Paul takes Nina out for a walk before lunch, usually half a mile to a mile. Nina is on a leash whenever she is outside. Paul cleans up after Nina.

12:45 p.m.: Paul and Nina return to the office. Paul cleans Nina's feet before she comes inside. Paul then eats his lunch.

1:00 p.m.: Paul has more meetings. Nina follows him around the office.

2:30 p.m.: Nina alerts Paul to the back doorbell by nudging him. After being nudged, Paul says, "Show me." Nina leads Paul to the back door. Paul rewards Nina. Nina goes back to her mat.

3:30 p.m.: Paul uses the restroom. Nina accompanies him.

5:15 p.m.: Paul takes Nina to a grassy area next to his office building and then cleans up after her.

5:30 p.m.: Paul buckles Nina into the car's back seat using her doggie seat belt. They come home.

Evening

6:00 p.m.: Nina has dinner. Three-quarters to a full cup of kibble. Paul refreshes her water bowl. Paul and Cate have a non-kibble dinner.

6:15 p.m.: Nina goes out to the fenced-in backyard to sniff around and patrol. Paul cleans her feet when she comes back inside.

7:00 p.m.: Paul, Cate, and Nina go to the grocery store. Paul buckles Nina into the back seat using her doggie seat belt.

7:15 p.m.: Paul and Cate look for their grocery items, accompanied by Nina. On every trip, the grocery store shoppers stop to ask questions about Nina. Cate answers the questions as best she can, thinking to herself that someday she really ought to write a book. Paul does not like to answer questions. Even though he has cochlear implants, the sounds of the grocery store refrigerators and overhead fans make it almost impossible for him to hear the questions.

8:30 p.m.: Paul buckles Nina into the back seat using her doggie seat belt. Paul, Cate, and Nina go home.

8:45 p.m.: Nina goes out to the fenced-in backyard to enjoy a sniffari and patrol. Paul throws the ball for her. Paul cleans Nina's feet when she comes back inside.

9:00 p.m.: Paul, Cate, and Nina go to bed. Nina sleeps in the middle of the bed. Paul and Cate sleep around her. Some nights the cat, Waldo, sleeps next to Nina and whaps her with his tail. Nina likes the attention.

Some Other Things about Nina (or Any Service Dog, for that Matter)

Nina is a service dog who is never off the clock. This is true for all hearing assist dogs. Some types of service dogs, such as guide dogs, have a strong notion of when they are and are not working. Such a dog knows he's off the clock when he's not in his harness leading his partner. But hearing assist dogs like Nina, diabetic alert dogs, and seizure assist dogs are taught to keep alert for the events that need a response. Sounds that Paul needs to hear can happen anytime. So Nina's always working.

Consequently, she goes with Paul pretty much everywhere, but there are four designated places she *cannot* go. The first is the dog park. The dog park is off limits because we don't know if the dogs there might be aggressive or have contagious illnesses. The second is the zoo. The zoo is forbidden because we don't want to upset the animals who live there by bringing in a dog. The animals in the zoo won't see a beloved, highly trained service dog. They'll only see a predator. The animals who are prey (such as deer) will see a threat, while the predators (such as lions) will see competition. We've heard stories about big cats hurling themselves against barriers and hurting themselves trying to get to a service dog. Third, Nina can't go into private homes without an invitation. Unlike public places, entrance into a private residence is not covered by federal law, so the Americans with Disabilities Act doesn't apply. Fourth, Nina cannot enter the likes of a church, mosque, or synagogue without being invited. Religious establishments aren't covered by federal law either, because of the separation of church and state. Even the federal ADA law cannot require a service animal to be invited into a church.

Now, there have been times when Nina was denied entrance to a place where ADA laws say she should be allowed. Our strategy in those instances is to simply leave. Life's too short to fight foolish battles. On a couple of occasions, Nina was denied entrance to a restaurant—a public place, mind you. The ADA requires public places to accept Nina. The first time, the manager explained why. Apparently, someone's dog that was wearing a service dog vest jumped on a table and ate another patron's meal. The dog then relieved itself in the middle of the restaurant. I suspect this was not a true service dog, but one of the aforementioned fakes. Nevertheless, we sympathized with the manager who was kind enough to offer us a table on the patio. We accepted. Later on, when the manager came to check on us, she was amazed that Nina vanished under the table. Actually, service dogs are trained to disappear as much as possible in public. We often alert the wait staff that Nina is under the table. Otherwise, she might surprise them by popping out when we're ready to leave. However, a business is not legally allowed to treat a service dog handler as inferior to other patrons, and we wouldn't have had to sit outside if we hadn't wanted to.

At another restaurant, we were denied entry because the owner was afraid that the health department would shut down her restaurant. We tried to explain the ADA laws to her, but she was not a native English speaker and the language barrier was too great to overcome. We were impressed to learn that this woman spoke four different languages, but we were unfortunately not fluent in anything offered in her linguistic buffet.

Overall, we try not to make a scene when we're denied entrance, even to a public place. There are always other options and we'll happily spend our money where we are all welcome. Most importantly, education in a compassionate manner is the focus because being an assistance dog team means being an ambassador for all teams.

Some Interesting ADA Stuff If You Happen to Own a Business

We've mentioned some of the ADA rules, but let's look a little closer at some of the more relevant and interesting requirements. Essentially, as with any ADA issue, most businesses have to make "reasonable modifications" to accommodate people with disabilities, and so that includes making modifications for service animals. If you have a "no pets" policy, you have to make an exception if someone enters with a service dog.

As discussed, people can (and do) sometimes take advantage of this to get their non-service animal in the door. Nevertheless, if it's your business, you only get to ask two questions about the animal: 1) is it required because of a disability? and 2) what work or task has it been trained to do? Assistance dog handlers are obligated to answer these two questions and nothing further. They don't have to disclose any personal/medical information. In other words, you can't ask for documentation or require the animal to perform.

If you're a hotel, you can't designate certain rooms for people with service animals, nor can you charge any additional fees. But a guest can't leave an animal in a room unattended, and they are still responsible for any damages an assistance dog may cause.

Beyond letting the animal into your business, you don't have to do much more. You have no obligation to care for or supervise the animal. You're not expected to make food or even water available. That's all on the owner. In fact, the ADA requires that the service animal

54

be under the control of its handler at all times. Bottom line: let the animal in. But if it ends up being disruptive, you're within your rights to request that the animal be removed from the premises.

Paul and I have traveled with Nina. We're limited on where we can take her because if she leaves the country, she might have to go into quarantine depending on the laws of that nation. Since we're unwilling to have her separated from Paul for any amount of time, most foreign travel is out. The one exception is our neighbors to the north. Canada is very welcoming of service dogs, and each province has specific public access allowances. As long as we have her medical, vaccination and dog license papers in order, they are happy to invite the pup in. We actually had more difficulty getting Nina back home to the USA. So… many… questions!

Please Ignore Service Dogs

Here's the thing about service dogs. They're fasci-
nating animals, and everybody seems to want to interact

with them. It's perfectly natural. You see a well-behaved dog with a vest leading, or, in some way, helping his partner, and you just can't resist. You want to approach and pet the dog. You want to ask all sorts of questions about him. You want to offer him a treat.

Please don't. Service dogs are born pleasers. If they weren't, they wouldn't be sufficiently trainable to be service dogs. For Nina's part, she'd spend all day seeking praise and treats by anyone who finds her an irresistibly "good dog." Who wouldn't prefer that to working?

But petting and attention distracts the service dog from doing their job. I know it doesn't look like she's doing much. She's just sitting there, looking around. Maybe she's trotting alongside Paul. But she's waiting to hear the sounds to which she was trained to alert Paul. Nina's only trained to respond to a handful of sounds. If she were trained to respond to every buzz and bell, she'd do nothing but nudge Paul constantly anytime the pair would find themselves in a big box store, like Target. Next time you're in one, listen closely. Every time a checkout cashier scans something, there is a beep. The PA system rings a bell before the announcements. Nina needs to be undistracted to be able to distinguish between these sounds and sounds she needs to alert Paul to, such as the fire alarm.

At home, for example, we have two kitchen timers in our kitchen. One of them is used exclusively by Paul. Nina has been trained to alert him when it goes off. The other one, which is built into the microwave, is the one I use. They sound very similar to us humans, but Nina *never* confuses them. We have had guests criticize her for not responding to the microwave but Nina knows that's not her sound.

So even though Nina looks like she's doing nothing, she's always on alert, listening for a smoke detector, a klaxon horn (the "ahoooga" kind), a fire bell, the ring tone of Paul's phone, his phone's message tones, the kitchen timer, the doorbell, a knock on the door, and a few others. When you pet her, she loses focus, or, rather, begins focusing on the attention you're giving her. Both Paul and I have seen this happen.

Types of Distractors

Are you a distractor? See if one of the following describes you.

The Aggressive Petter

Recently, we went to a government office and were filling out some paperwork. Suddenly, a woman came running down the hall yelling, "Dooooooooooooooooggg!" She burst into the room and sat on the floor next to Nina where she talked to her excitedly, rubbing her vigorously. Nina rolled onto her back for belly rubs, then started to jump around to play.

"Nina is a working dog," I announced.

"Oh, I don't mind," the woman replied. "It doesn't bother me none!"

The woman continued to rub Nina with gusto.

"She is working now," I said.

The woman was so into rubbing Nina, she ignored me. Fortunately, the clerk who was helping us with the paperwork was this woman's boss and asked her to leave, although she had to repeat the request several times. The woman seemed confused and almost defiant, but she eventually went back down the hall to her desk. It took a little while for Paul to refocus and calm Nina, and we spent twice as long on the paperwork as we otherwise would have.

This happens more often than you might imagine. Aggressive petters walk up to Nina and pet her with almost unconscious movements, obviously giving no thought as to why a dog would be in an environment where dogs usually aren't. Sometimes it's children, but mostly it's adults. Typically, these people talk to us while they're petting Nina, rarely letting us get a word in edgewise. Our requests to not pet the service dog don't register in their brains.

The Cuddler

Sometimes people want to cuddle Nina. Hey, we've all been there. You're having a rough day and suddenly there's a dog in the picture and you want to throw your arms around her and get a comforting, furry hug. But out in public with her bandana on, Nina is working. She knows that work time is not cuddle time. Besides, Nina is not an emotional support dog. She's not here to make you feel better, even though we can certainly appreciate the comfort a dog can provide.

The Rewarder

People are sometimes tempted to actually reward a stranger's service dog for being, well, a service dog. I'm reminded of a YouTube video I saw a few years back. It was a commercial from the Norwegian Association of the Blind called "Don't Disturb the Ones Working" where two women walked up to a road construction worker and cooed, "What a cutie!" The theme was repeated a few times with variations, such as people praising the supermarket cashier for doing a good job after every item she scanned. One man tried to play ball with the bus driver while the bus was speeding down the highway. A man hugged a builder who was trying to install a picture window while enthusiastically telling him he was "a good boy."

I love that ad because it showed the strong human desire to reward a hero. There is something overwhelming in the desire to cheer on the good guys, a feeling that's magnified when you see it in person. Of course, Paul and I agree that Nina *is* amazing. On the other hand, like the firefighter and the cop, she's just doing her job. Nina accompanying Paul to the grocery store is our everyday life. Please let them both work uninterrupted.

The Dog Talker

Closely related to the Rewarder is the Dog Talker. These are people who chat openly with the service dog as though they are old friends. Many of these people are confident in their "canine charisma." Dogs just plain like them, and they love to flex their powers. Not long ago, Paul and I were in a doctor's waiting room when the nurse came out to call the next patients, an elderly man and his wife, both with mobility issues. They struggled to get out of their chairs and make their way into the office, which the nurse would have noticed had she not first seen Nina and decided to become engrossed in conversation with her. "Who's a good dog? You are! Oh yes, you are! Oh yes you are!" Paul and I, who the nurse was as oblivious to as the elderly couple, looked on as the receptionist left her desk to help the poor couple into the doctor's office. For a full five minutes, the nurse continued chatting with Nina. "You're a good dog! Oh yes, you are!" Eventually, the receptionist had to prod the nurse to get back to work and she reluctantly ended her conversation with her old friend Nina, hopeful, no doubt, that they would see each other again very, very soon.

The Treater

Along those lines, please don't try to feed a service dog a treat. Where Nina is concerned, only Paul can feed her. This task is part of the continuous bonding of the service dog team. It's a very important part of their partnership. Paul must be seen as the source of everything that's good in Nina's life. Basically, she needs to love him the best. Service dogs will only work for love. If she can get treats from someone else, Nina will look for other strategies for rewards and those strategies might not involve her doing her job. We can't afford to undo her training.

Miscellaneous Distractors

Other distractions we have seen: people who want to take selfies with Nina. This reminds me of those "swim with the dolphins adventures" you see in Florida and other coastal states. You pay money to swim with the dolphins and the water park has a photographer who takes a ton of pictures. They then sell you the overpriced pictures so you can post them on Facebook to impress your friends. I actually did this several years ago with my eighty-year-old mother. She was graceful and calm in the water. She was Esther Williams, waving at the camera while holding on to a dolphin fin. Me, I was more like Lou Costello meets the Creature from the Black Lagoon. Dolphins are enormous and alien up close!

Please don't be a distractor. Nina is not an amusement, an attraction, a toy, or a prop. She is a working service dog.

She is also not a show dog. We ask that you not try to command her. And she is not here to perform tricks or take selfies with strangers.

Nina is here to help Paul with his hearing disability.

Speaking of Nina

Sometimes people want to ask a slew of questions about Nina in her role as a service dog. Typically, I deliver an elevator speech about hearing assist dogs and what they do. If the generous deaf woman with her corgi hadn't launched into her canned explanation of hearing assist dogs many years ago, we wouldn't have Nina. With every speech, I feel I'm paying her gift forward. This book is also a way to pay it forward.

For the most part, however, I confess I appreciate it when people keep their questions to themselves, or go home and use Google for the answers. (Or read books like the one you're holding.) I especially appreciate it when people don't ask Paul their questions. My husband is not only deaf, but he's an introvert. Yes, he has cochlear implants which are hearing-assist devices, but conversation is still difficult for him. Mostly it's environmental factors that make conversations a challenge. Background sounds are all around us. Those of us with the ability to hear have had a lifetime of practice focusing on certain sounds and ignoring the rest. We filter out the large fans above us in the grocery stores or the hum of the restaurant air conditioner. Hearing assist devices don't filter out any background sounds so when Paul is in a public place, he has to really focus on what you say to him. He has to concentrate. Kids will often talk softly with their heads turned or their hands over their mouths, making themselves difficult to hear. Finally, if he is outside, even the slightest wind will interfere with his cochlear implants. Because Paul went deaf as an adult and has very normal speech patterns, most people don't recognize that Paul struggles to hear.

As for me, I'm more talkative in public, and I can hear. Still, that doesn't mean I necessarily want the battle-field promotion. Nonetheless, I find myself soften when kids come along asking questions, showing curiosity and a desire to want to explore their world. Sometimes I'll stray from the elevator speech. I love questions like, "Can your dog talk to you?" "Did you find this dog or did this dog find you?" "Did your dog go to school to be a good dog?" We're happy when our presence introduces children to a new social situation. I'll answer their questions, but then we cross our fingers hoping the line of questioning doesn't morph into a full-blown seminar. We're not a roving band of educators waiting to enlighten the world. We just want to get home before our ice cream melts.

We've been asked before if Nina can be made available for presentations about service dogs. Well, yes, but not Nina alone. Paul and Nina are inseparable, as it should be. For a full presentation, you'll get all three of us. I do the talking, Paul demonstrates what Nina can do, and Nina is just her amazing self. We occasionally do public speaking gigs to raise money for Can Do Canines. Since they give service dogs to people with disabilities at no cost, we feel this is the least we can do. Just recently, we finally raised enough money to repay Can Do Canines for the cost of training Nina. That was approximately $25,000. This is more than my car is worth, but Nina's value is immeasurable. Our next goal is to eventually raise enough money to pay for Paul's next service dog.

We have also presented to firefighters about service dogs. Paul happens to drive a firetruck (and is not the only deaf firefighter in our community, proving that deaf people can do anything that hearing people can do except hear) and did most of the talking to that group. It's important that first responders know what to do with a service dog in the event that the partner is unable to care for it. The short answer is that they should look for the family and friends of the service dog partner. If they can't be found in a timely manner, then the first responders should contact the service dog agency listed on the dog tags or cape. Finally, if friends, family, and the service dog agency are all unreachable, then they should give the dog to the sheriff to deliver to an animal shelter.

Additionally, we have some friends who teach college, and we'll sometimes talk to their classes. I particularly like to talk to graduate-level counseling and social work classes. These classes are filled with people who might end up advocating for people with disabilities. These students might help improve a life by recommending a service dog someday.

Often times, when we're out with Nina, we'll get a reaction that runs along these lines: "Your service dog reminds me of my old dog. Can I tell you about him?" Sometimes the person will wait for an answer, but most times they'll just launch into a story. Sometimes the story is about how their dog passed away recently, or how they miss a dog from their childhood. I'm amused when people tell me that Nina, a small black lab, reminds them of their Pomeranian or Bernese Mountain Dog. My guess is they see the unconditional love Nina has towards Paul and it makes them think of their loving pup.

Of all the behaviors a stranger might do, the best choice, beyond ignoring the service dog, is to talk about dogs and love. I usually end these conversations with, "Thank you for your story and kind words." I like the stories because those telling them are not distracting Nina from her work. Instead they're just offering a happy sliver of their life.

Overall, when it comes to interacting with a service dog in public, it's a simple enough proposition. Please ignore service dogs. The best thing you can do is carry on with your day. For Paul and me, we'd be grateful if Nina was not distracted. If you feel the need to talk about the dog, maybe you could share your thoughts with whomever you're with as you walk on by. That way, everyone can finish their grocery shopping in time for dinner.

Frequently Asked Questions

If you still have any questions about service dogs (or Nina, in particular) you might find the answers here. These are some of the more common questions that Paul and I have been asked.

Can your service dog sniff out bombs or cancer?
No. Service dogs are trained for specific tasks to help a single disabled individual.

How do you know how to take care of your service dog?
In our case, Can Do Canines gave us a big binder with everything we need to know about caring for Nina. It included information about feeding, weight, what to do with the dog if you are hospitalized, legal information, on-going training, and so on.

Does Nina like men or women better?
When we first met Nina, she bounded across the room and immediately ran to me. The trainers called her and sent her to Paul but she would always return to me. When we asked why, we were informed that Nina's puppy raiser was a woman, she was trained in a woman's prison, and all of her trainers were women. Nina

naturally assumed that I was to be her partner. Nina's trainer asked me to ignore Nina for about a half of a year. My heart sank when I heard that. When I asked why, the trainer said, "You can be happy she is near and snuggle at night but keep your distance until Paul and Nina build their partnership." I then asked, "What am I, furniture?" "No. You are happy furniture," the trainer replied.

It was a relief when Paul and Nina fully bonded and I could return as a full family member and not just a cheery ottoman.

Was Nina really trained in prison?

Yes. She was trained in a woman's prison in Wisconsin for many months. Prison training is helpful to both the service dog training organizations and for the prisoners. Prisoners have plenty of time to train the dogs and can give them the attention they need for a proper education. The prisoners learn new skills and get the dog's unconditional love. If you want to watch a video that will make your heart melt, look up Internet videos of prisoner and service dog reunions.

Can you show me a service dog trick?

No. Service dogs do not exist for your amusement. The ADA specifically states that service dogs are never required to demonstrate their tasks.

Can you feed a service dog a hot dog?
(asked by a five-year-old boy)

Sorry, no. Nina only eats kibble that is approved by Can Do Canines and provided by Paul. Following their standards, she can only eat a high protein kibble supplemented with fish oil and glucosamine. The approved companies are from the USA. She is not permitted to eat imported dog foods due to quality issues.

Nina's life seems kind of dull.

Is that a question?

Well…is it?

Maybe by human standards. Nina sleeps most of the day. Her job is to wait for specific sounds. I guess it is boring being a service dog, but she provides a vital function.

Why don't you let Nina have any fun?

We do. Nina has a fenced-in yard where she can be off the leash. The minimum size and the height of the fenced-in area were all dictated by her training organization, Can Do Canines. She has a half acre to roam and explore. Inside, she has a big basket of toys and her kennel, where she feels safe. She also has her own spot on the sofa with a special blanket to snuggle in when she sleeps through the movies we watch. We usually mute the parts of the movies when animals growl. Nina hates those parts.

Will she play fetch?

Nina is a Labrador retriever. She *loves* to play fetch. If you throw her tennis ball in the water, however, she will stand on the shore and wait until you get it. A girl has to have standards, you see.

Where does Nina sleep?

For his fiftieth birthday I promised Paul I would not complain if his next dog slept on the bed with him. As an adult, I am not a huge fan of dogs in the bed. Paul was delighted with his gift. He adores sleeping with dogs. I have slowly come around. At night Nina sleeps in the middle of our bed. Sometimes she's near our heads, but mostly at waist height. She usually points her nose toward the bedroom door, but not always. I like to snuggle her butt. I know it sounds gross, but Nina has a large thick tail, which her vet calls an otter tail. So, I don't come in contact with anything unpleasant when I snuggle her butt. This also ensures I don't have kicking feet aimed at me when she runs in her sleep. When we're home during the day, Nina sleeps on the sofa.

Does your service dog hunt?

Nope. Nina was not bred or trained to hunt. She's not aggressive enough to hunt, anyway, and doesn't like to get wet. She'd be confused if she went hunting. Plus, she dislikes loud noises.

So, Nina does not know anything about guns?

Well, as a matter of fact, one evening, Paul found a Nerf gun among some old toys. He snuck up and shot me. Of course, the Nerf dart merely bounced off me, and we both laughed. Nina, however, did not find this funny at all. She came to comfort me and ignored Paul for the rest of the day. I got all the snuggles that night. She even ignored Paul when he tried to make it up to her. The next day, when they started their workday together, she was still a little miffed at him. By the time they got home, she had forgiven him. We hid the Nerf gun and it has never come out of the cabinet again.

What is it like having a service dog?

For Paul, it's as if he's adopted a two-year-old who will never grow up. He makes sure she's fed, calms her, wipes her muddy paws, cleans up after her, and rewards her when she is good. He carries a bag with all of her supplies everywhere he goes.

What do you take with you when you go out with Nina?

Paul uses a fanny pack which includes everything he needs to care for Nina away from home. I call it his doggy diaper bag. It has two bottle holders. In one bottle holder, Paul keeps a cup with treats in it to reward Nina when she does a good job. In the other bottle holder, he keeps a bottle of clean water specifically for Nina. He also keeps poop bags, a towel, a tennis ball, paw wax for protecting Nina's paws from salt and snow in the winter, baby wipes for cleaning muddy paws, one meal in case they can't get home in time for dinner, a collapsible bowl for dinner or water, the Paul and Nina service dog team identity card, cards which explain ADA service dog laws, and information cards about Can Do Canines for people who want to learn more about service dogs.

What do you do with Nina when Paul has to go to the bathroom?

Nina usually follows Paul into the men's room. If they're in a public place, Paul leads Nina into the stall with him. Sometimes at restaurants, Paul asks a specific friend or family member at the table to watch Nina when he goes to the bathroom. He then hands the friend or family member the leash. At home, Nina sleeps on the sofa while Paul is in the bathroom. When I'm at home, Waldo the kitty insists on joining me in the bathroom. Is this too much information?

Is Waldo a service animal?

Not in a strict definitional sense. Nina, as it happens, is very sensitive to scolding. Waldo, on the other hand, doesn't care one bit what you say to him as long as you're giving him some sort of attention when he wants it. So

Waldo's de facto service has been to accept all blame for most household disturbances including spills, farting, and disruption of internet service. The latter offense, losing the internet, has actually been Waldo's fault many times. He has an addiction to chewing on thicker cables like the internet coaxial cable. In all instances, Waldo is unrepentant and denies all wrongdoing. He denies it even when you catch him in the act. Lately, Paul has been calling Waldo "kittiot," a portmanteau of "kitty" and "idiot."

Can cats be service animals?

Waldo would answer this question with a look that says, *You can't be serious.* However, we've all seen the charming YouTube videos where cats have been trained to run obstacle courses, retrieve items, and even do sophisticated ballet routines with their owners. Trainable cats have an unusual combination of traits including intelligence, food motivation, and a low rate of narcissism. But overall, dogs are eminently more trainable than cats.

Waldo, for example, is not at all motivated by the promise of food. When he is frightened, he is a champ at hiding. That is how he got his name. And he does not want to leave the house. Moreover, he has never exhibited even the slightest interest in being helpful in any way.

If Nina is a metaphorical two-year-old, Waldo is a metaphorical senior citizen who is sick of our crap.

When he sees a robin through the window, he chitters at him as if he is saying, "Get off my lawn."

Does Nina get along with Waldo?

Nina loves cats. Waldo, on the other hand, merely tolerates Nina. Paul thought it would be funny to train Nina to nudge Waldo with her nose whenever the command "Where's Waldo?" was issued. So that's what she does. This actually came in handy one time when, as it happens, we really didn't know where Waldo was. Waldo is an indoor cat and somehow managed to escape from the garage, slipping, unbeknownst to us, into our enclosed backyard. A whole day went by with Paul and I looking everywhere for Waldo.

We consulted a veterinarian's website that said that some indoor cats get so freaked out when they are outside that you can walk right past them while calling them and they still remain hidden. It also said that cats will get thirsty before they get hungry, so a bowl of water might attract the cat. This was good because we certainly didn't want to put food out that might attract coyotes or raccoons. The next morning, while out in the backyard for her post-breakfast constitutional, Nina was observed by Paul to be fascinated by something under the picnic table. Paul couldn't quite see what, until Nina relentlessly nudged Waldo out from under the table where Paul grabbed him and brought him inside to me. Later, we followed the tracks from the picnic table to discover that Waldo had apparently been hiding the whole time under the gazebo with our resident colony of bunnies.

Were any of the bunnies hurt?

Waldo was ravenous when he came back in and was quite clean, so we've concluded that no bunnies were harmed by Waldo's presence.

Speaking of different animals, are there other true service animals besides dogs?

Believe it or not, there are service horses for people who do not want or cannot use a dog. One of the first organizations to train service horses was The Guide Horse Foundation, which was founded in 1999. Since then, more service horse training organizations have appeared. There are several advantages to using a horse, rather than a dog. Miniature horses, with an average lifespan of thirty years, live almost twice as long as most dogs. For those allergic to or frightened of dogs a horse makes a good alternative.

One huge general advantage with a guide horse is that horses have excellent vision. With eyes placed on the sides of their heads, they possess nearly 350-degree vision, are sensitive to motion in their field of vision, and often detect a potential hazard before their sighted trainers. They also have excellent night vision and can see clearly in almost total darkness.

However, while a dog can adapt to many different home situations, a horse must live outdoors, requiring a shelter and room to move about when not on duty. Of course, they're difficult if not impossible to take on limited-space public transportation.

Getting back to Nina: what's her favorite person/ food/activity?

Hands down, Paul is Nina's favorite person because she was taught that all good things come from him. Unless Paul is very sick, only he is allowed to feed and care for Nina. I feed her, on average, only about once a year.

Her favorite food is cheese. In training, this is called a "high value" treat. If Nina is growing bored of training, or not motivated to keep working, she will often perk up and work harder if we offer cheese as the high value reward.

Her favorite activity is romping in the snow. It's odd; she loves snow, but dislikes rain and water. When it snows, she swims from snowbank to snowbank like a circus seal. She also loves tennis balls and being scratched right behind the ears. Also, if you start to dance, she'll get on her hind legs and dance with you. Makes no difference if there's music playing or not. She also loves breakfast and supper. She does *not* like Daylight Savings Time because it throws off her internal mealtime clock.

Does Nina ever growl at you?

Nina has never growled at us. In fact, I don't recall ever hearing her growl.

Does she bark?

She can bark but generally doesn't. The first time I heard her bark, about four months after we got her, I was alarmed. The sun had set, and she was outside on her usual evening sniffari (a sniffing safari). I heard a deep throated WOOF. At first, I was confused because it seemed to be too deep of a voice for our small lab. And yet it was definitely her. I grabbed Paul's hand and dragged him out the back door. We both started to call for Nina. Soon we spotted her staring down a raccoon on the other side of the fence. Actually, to call it a raccoon would be an understatement. This thing was at least forty-five pounds, basically the size of Nina. We named it the Trash Panda. We had trouble catching it because even the largest trap our exterminator put out was barely big enough. But eventually, we caught the Trash Panda and relocated him to Sheboygan, Wisconsin.

When Nina is outside, we always keep an eye on her. We also keep the backyard lit up at night. Nina has seen other animals, such as possums and deer. We don't want Nina meeting any outdoor animals. The good news is that she'll come when called in any situation.

Is Nina allowed on the furniture?

Yes and no. In our house, we allow her to sit on the sofa and bed. In other houses, she knows not to go on the furniture unless she is invited.

Can Nina dress up for Halloween?

Yes and no. Owners can dress up their service dogs, but we don't dress up Nina. She doesn't like to wear anything. For service dog purposes, Nina's line is bred for calmness, intelligence, food motivation, and smaller size. Inadvertently, touch sensitivity has been bred into her family, as well. As a consequence, Nina prefers wearing nothing at all. When a full-size service dog cape is put on her, she lays down and whimpers. She seems okay with her collar and her service bandana. She dislikes wearing a doggy seatbelt but she has to anyway.

What does your service dog want to do, but you won't let her do?

With Nina, it's three things: vacuum the kitchen floor with her tongue, lick the dishes clean in the dishwasher, and beg everyone she meets for treats and affection.

Do you force Nina to do her job?

No one can force a service dog to do her job. They do it out of pure love. If it's too hard to get a service dog to work, they're usually placed as a pet. Oddly enough, if a service dog in training is too friendly, and it interferes with her work, she might not graduate the service dog program.

Do you love your service dog like a pet?

We love her more than a pet because she keeps Paul safe.

A Transition in
Three Conversations

Act 1: Before we Knew about Hearing Assist Dogs.

Paul: We need to move so I can get a dog.

Cate: Move? Are you crazy? This is a 100-year-old condo. I love it here. Look at the architectural details. Look at that crown molding. This is my home.

Paul: That's fine but it is not mine. I am shoehorned in here. I miss my stuff. Besides, wouldn't be nice to have a place to make art?

Cate: Yeah. That would be great.

Paul: And air conditioning?

Cate: Oh, yeah, big boy. Talk Aprilaire porn to me.

Paul: And a dog?

Cate: Okay, but dogs live outside.

Paul: No, they don't.

Cate: All of my father's hunting dogs lived outside. That's why we always had two. That way they could play with each other, snuggle, and keep each other company.

Paul: I'll keep the dog company.

Cate: So you're going to live outside? I'll miss you, but if you must…

Paul: No. The dog will live inside with us. Chief lived inside my house.

Cate: True, but if possession is nine tenths of the law, then technically you lived in Chief's house… his hillbilly shack to be precise.

Paul: It was not that bad.

Cate (in her best Bullwinkle voice): Hey Rocky, watch me pull a black lab out of a crack in this sofa. Nothing up my sleeve…presto.

Paul: Okay, I get it. Chief shed a lot.

Cate: A lot is an understatement. Let me lift this cushion. See? If you have a spinning wheel, we can get my mother to knit you another Chief.

Paul: I miss Chief. He was my best friend.

Cate: I know.

(*Brief Silence*)

Cate: Do you remember the day that Chief pushed me out of your bed?

Paul: You were in his spot.

Cate: I then crawled into the other side of the bed and he pushed me out again.

Paul: The whole bed was his spot.

Cate: He gave you a tiny corner to sleep in.

Paul: He was my blanket and pillow. I was always warm.

Cate: New topic. What will you name your two dogs?

Paul: Something funny and unusual.

Cate: I suggest Hello Kitty and My Little Pony.

Paul: No. That is not funny. That's weird. You are such a weirdo.

Cate: I think we have different definitions of both funny and unusual. Besides, who's the weirdo? Mr. I-won't-eat-anything-green? Okay, what is funny to you?

Paul: Comedians? Help me think of some.

Cate: Groucho, Chico, and Harpo Marx? Stephen Wright? Jerry Seinfeld? Mary Tyler Moore? Paula Poundstone?

Paul: I loved Abbot and Costello as a kid. I am going to name them Bud and Lou. Woof.

Cate: Meow.

Act 2: After we were Accepted for a Hearing Assist Dog.

Cate: Do you think you get to name your hearing assist dog?

Paul: Dora said that the dogs are smart and we can train him to accept a nickname.

Cate: So what are you going to name it?

Paul: Bud.

Cate: Not Lou? Lou Costello was the funny one. Bud Abbot was just the straight man.

Paul: The dog will be my new ear bud. He will be Bud.

Cate: What if your dog is a female?

Paul: Ummmm… Rosebud. Woof.

Cate: Woof.

Act 3: Immediately After a Service Dog Joined our Family.

Cate: Are you going to train Nina to answer to Bud?

Paul: No, Nina is a good name.

Cate: Particularly paired with your last name. Hey, would you give her the last name Menasha? Nina Menasha!

Paul: No. Rename the cat Menasha if you want to tell that joke daily.

Cate: But Waldo fits the cat too well. Look at him, he is such a Waldo! Plus he is hard to find. You know his name is registered at the vet as Waldo Sheboygan, like the sign on North Highway 43.

Paul: Sigh.

Cate: Sarah, one of the trainers, calls your dog Nina Beans.

Paul: I know, what's up with that?

Cate: Exactly. Particularly since Nina Boo makes much more sense.

Paul: Have you heard her contented sigh? Her name should be Nina Moo.

Cate and Paul (together): Moooooooooooo.

Bibliography and Recommended Books

Barnett, S. (2002). Communication with deaf and hard-of-hearing people: A guide for medical education. *Academic Medicine, 77*(7), 694-700.

Braham, J. (2012) *Another Language: Portraits of Assistance Dogs and Their People*. Peterbough, N.H.: Bauhan Publishing.

Bulletin: *Frequently Asked Questions about Service Animals and the ADA*, U.S. Department of Justice, Civil Rights Division, Disability Rights Section, July 2011, web: *https://www.ada.gov/regs2010/service_animal_qa.html*.

Davis, M., and Bunnell, M. (2007) *Working Like Dogs: The Service Dog Guidebook*. Crawford, Co.: Alpine Publications.

Dobbs Gross, P. (2006) *The Golden Bridge: A Guide to Assistance Dogs for Children Challenged by Autism or Other Developmental Disabilities*. West Lafayette, IN: Purdue University Press.

Duffy, K., and Mumford, L. (2011) *Partners with Paws: Service Dogs and the Lives They Change*. Happy Tail Books.

Eames, E., and Eames, T. (2004) *Partners in Independence: A Success Story of Dogs and the Disabled*. Mechanicsburg, PA: Barkleigh, Productions.

Goodavage, M. (2019). *Doctor Dogs: How our Best Friends are Becoming our Best Medicine.* Hialeah, Florida: Dutton Press.

Juatai, J. (2018) *Post Traumatic Stress Disorder and the Service Dog.* Booklocker.

Juatai, J. and Nemitz, K. (2020) *Why is That Doggie in the Store?* Independently Published.

Lieu, C., Sadler, G., Fullerton, J., and Deyo Stohlmann, P. (2007) Communication Strategies for Nurses Interacting With Patients Who Are Deaf. *Dermatology Nursing,* 19(6):541-544; 549-55.

Marcus, D. (2011) *The Power of Wagging Tails: A Doctor's Guide to Dog Therapy and Healing.* New York, N.Y.: DemosHealth Publications.

Montalvan, L.C., and Witter, B. (2014) *Tuesday Tucks Me In: The Loyal Bond between a Soldier and his Service Dog.* New York, N.Y.: Roaring Brook Press.

Nimmer, K. (2010) *Two Plus Four Equals One: Celebrating the Partnership of People with Disabilities and Their Assistance Dogs.* Indianapolis, IN: Dog Ear Publishing.

Ring, E. (1993) *Assistance Dogs: In Special Service.* Brookfield, Connecticut: The Millbrook Press.

www.ingramcontent.com/pod-product-compliance
Lightning Source LLC
Chambersburg PA
CBHW070027030426

42335CB00017B/2319